A BOTTLE COLLECTORS' GUIDE
European Seals, Case Gins & Bitters

By the same author

Bottle Collecting

Treasure Hunting For All

Digging Up Antiques

Collecting Pot Lids

A Treasure Hunter's Guide

International Bottle Collecting

Fletcher's Non-Dating Bottle Price Guide

Bottles In Colour

Tomorrow's Antiques

How To Live At Half The Price

Two sealed wine bottles of a shape
popular in the United States in
the late nineteenth century.
Unlike free-blown 'onion' bottles
these specimens were blown in
metal moulds.

The bottles shown in the photograph
are from the stocks of Standen
Antiques, Standen House, Chute
Standen, Andover, Hampshire,
England.

A BOTTLE COLLECTORS' GUIDE

EUROPEAN SEALS, CASE GINS AND BITTERS

EDWARD FLETCHER

LATIMER

First published in 1976
by Latimer New Dimensions Limited
14 West Central Street, London WC1A 1JH

SBN 901539 47 3

Designed with the help of the students of the Graphic
Design Course at the Harlow Technical College

Typeset by Mason & Weldon Ltd, London: printed in
Great Britain by The Anchor Press Ltd, and bound by
William Brendon & Son Ltd, both of Tiptree, Essex

CONTENTS

INTRODUCTION

In addition to a common language and a shared enthusiasm for digging holes in the ground, bottle collectors in the United States, Canada, Britain, Australia, New Zealand, and South Africa have in their collections many bottles which can be found in the unexplored nineteenth-century refuse dumps in all six countries. This common heritage of empties — the majority of which once contained wine, whisky, gin, and other alcoholic beverages — happens to include some of the most prized collectable bottles, a coincidence that has done more to promote international trade within the fraternity than has our common mother tongue. Examine the bottles proudly displayed by a collector in New York, Montreal, London, Sydney, Wellington or Johannesburg and you will find an international assortment: French, Spanish and Portuguese wines, Dutch case gins, Scotch and Irish whiskies, German liqueurs, English bitters — all of them relics of an age when Europe was the factory (and distillery) of the world and the cargo of every sailing ship leaving a European port to make the perilous trans-Atlantic or equatorial journey included hand and mould-blown bottles with shoulder seals or pictorial embossing.

Although some of these bottles have been described and illustrated in books on bottle collecting published in most of the above countries no writer has yet attempted a book to help collectors identify and date their European specimens. The reason for this obvious gap in bottle collectors' literature is that in the United States, where bottle collecting first became a popular hobby and where most books on the subject have been published, historical records relating to European bottles are almost non-existent. Fortunately the remainder of the bottle collecting fraternity — especially the British contingent — has recently begun to take a greater interest in publishing historical information and it is with the hope of satisfying a need felt by all bottle collectors in the aforementioned countries that I offer this guide to nineteenth-century European seals, case gins, and bitters. It illustrates the seals and trade marks of approximately five hundred English, Scottish, Irish, Dutch, French, German,

Spanish and Portuguese companies known to have sold whisky, gin, wine and bitters to an international market in the nineteenth century. Research sources consulted include British trade marks records, nineteenth-century British, Australian and American newspapers, and the records of The British Bottle Collectors Club. These sources have in many cases enabled me to provide the name and address of the company which used a particular trade mark or seal and the date from which the mark or seal was first used or first registered as a trade mark in Britain. With this information and the notes on the evolution of European bottle shapes and designs it should be possible to date to within a few years most of the European bottles found in collections throughout the world.

At the present time the number of published books on bottle collecting by British writers amounts to less than a dozen. We have far to go to match the prodigious output of more than two hundred books on the subject written by our American cousins; but a start has been made and I am convinced the wealth of historical research sources available in Britain will ensure a flow of literature of interest to bottle collectors everywhere. It has been my privilege to lead the British bottle collecting fraternity for several years, as founder of The British Bottle Collectors Club, as editor of the magazine, *Bottles and Relics News*, and as author of the books which first brought the hobby to popularity in Britain. Much of my early knowledge about the subject was gained from books written by enthusiasts in other countries. I hope this book will prove as useful to them as their books were to me.

Edward Fletcher
104 Harwal Road,
Redcar, Cleveland, England.

HOW TO USE THIS BOOK

The seals listed are in date order and divided into five groups: pre-1820, 1820—40, 1841—60, 1861—80, post-1880. A bottle's body shape and the position of the seal on the bottle will provide the first clues to its approximate age. When looking for a seal in the relevant section bear in mind that it is likely that some bottles will carry seals which differ slightly from the illustrations. Words or letters may be missing, or only part of the complete trade mark may have been used on the seal. If you are unable to find a particular seal in the group you are checking turn to the index at the back of the book where you will find listings (and page numbers) under various headings including animals, birds, etc. Look for your seal under the appropriate heading and check the pages indicated.

If the seal you are looking for is not illustrated in the book, and if it bears a company name (or initials) turn to the pages where I have listed advertisers whose bottled drinks were mentioned in newspaper advertisements between 1850 and 1880. If the name on the seal appears in one of these lists you will know *approximately* when such bottles were in use. If after checking illustrations, index and lists of advertisers you still cannot find the seal or a reference to the company which used it please send a photograph or drawing of the seal together with details of the bottle's shape and colour and any information you have on the bottle's history, to me at the address shown on p7. I hope to include details of all seals sent to me by readers in a future edition of this book.

Readers who wish to carry out further research after finding a reference to a particular seal in the book should note that the company address and other information given alongside each illustration are quoted verbatim from the records I consulted when compiling the book. Additional information (where the record seemed to need clarification) is shown in square brackets. Where a date is preceded by the words 'first used' I am quoting the original trade mark registration documents which requested each applicant to state the year in which the mark was first used. If a registration date only is quoted the applicant made no claim to use of the mark before that date. If a date is preceded by the words 'in use' this indicates a year in which the mark was used but not necessarily the *first* year in which it was used.

1. SEALED BOTTLES

The practice of applying a hot pad of glass to the body of a newly-blown bottle and impressing an identification mark into the pad before the glass cools is an ancient one which can be traced back at least as far as the second century. But it was not until the mid seventeenth century, when glass replaced stoneware in the manufacture of wine bottles, that the use of these glass pads — or seals — began to spread throughout Europe. Only the rich could afford to buy glass wine bottles when they first appeared and for this reason the earliest seals bear the coats-of-arms of great nobles who ordered bottles by the dozen from glass manufacturers for use in their wine-cellars and as decanters to be passed round the table at mealtimes. Within a few years the middle classes were able to imitate their betters as bottles became less expensive; Pepys records in his diary that in 1663 he 'went to the Mitre' to see wine put into his 'crested bottles'. By 1750 many wine merchants were offering customers a variety of alcoholic drinks in bottles bearing seals impressed with names and trade marks, though the bottles remained the property of the wine merchants whose seals they carried and to whom they were returned for re-filling whenever necessary. In Britain some whisky distillers and a small number of brewers also began to use sealed bottles in the mid eighteenth century. The distillers had their names and trade marks impressed on their seals, but the majority of brewers had their seals marked only with the bottle's capacity.

In continental Europe the use of sealed bottles also achieved widespread popularity in the eighteenth century, especially in Holland where vast quantities of Dutch gin — known as Hollands or Geneva — were bottled for export to all parts of the world in square 'case bottles' which were packaged for greater safety during shipment in wooden crates or cases. (See next section.) In France, Spain, Portugal, Germany and Italy, noblemen, the middle classes, wine growers, and merchants were all bottling their wines and liqueurs in sealed bottles before the end of the eighteenth century.

Until the recent explosion of interest in bottle collecting in Britain — where the hobby was imported from the United States in 1970 — it was generally accepted by museums and antique collectors that the sealed bottle era came to an end soon after 1850; that the practice gave way at about that time to embossing and to paper labels. Evidence which seemed to confirm this date came from museum catalogues and inventories of private collections which showed that very few sealed bottles in any collection could be dated later than 1850. However, evidence now being brought to light by the digging forks of fifty thousand British enthusiasts who have concentrated their activities on late Victorian refuse dumps clearly shows that it was *not* the making of sealed bottles which ended in 1850 but the practice of keeping them for re-use in one's cellars where they could be found by future antique collectors. After 1850 the bottles became so inexpensive they were simply thrown away when empty. These late Victorian seals do not carry the coats-of-arms or monograms of private individuals. They show the trade marks of wine and spirit merchants, shippers, growers, distillers, and manufacturers who carried on the business of selling alcoholic drinks to a thirsty public and who used seals *in addition* to paper labels. Their bottles have been found throughout the world wherever enthusiasts have excavated old refuse dumps and examples can be seen in most collections in Britain, North America, and Australia.

Because paper labels do not survive long burial in the ground and because the trade marks found on late-nineteenth-century seals rarely include the names and addresses of merchants and manufacturers collectors often experience difficulty when it comes to identifying and dating specimens. This is especially so in the United States where historical records relating to nineteenth-century European companies are not readily available. Fortunately members of The British Bottle Collectors Club have also taken a great interest in the histories of their sealed bottle finds and the results of their efforts in this field are recorded in the club's research files. Much of the information has come from trade marks records found during searches of the Trade Marks Registry in London where the marks of all British companies and those of foreign companies trading in Britain have been recorded since 1875. The entries on the register include, in addition to the trade mark and the name and address of the company, the date when a mark was first used. With this information it is possible to attribute many bottles bearing only pictorial seals (or pictorial embossing on later specimens) to a particular company and it is these records which have been gathered together for publication in this book.

Unfortunately it is not possible to compile a totally comprehensive list of all seals used in the late nineteenth century because some merchants and manufacturers simply registered their names as their trade marks and used unregistered designs on their seals. Some of these unregistered designs referred to a particular *brand* of alcoholic drink made by a company. For example: a firm trading as Andrew Johnson & Son of London might have registered the name A. Johnson & Son as a trade mark and then sold 'Johnson's Bull's Head Brand Gin' in bottles with a seal showing a bull's head. Without the paper label such a bottle would be difficult to identify, though the seal *might* also include the initials 'A.J.' or the word 'London' which would help to narrow the field of possibilities. Without these additional clues it is necessary to search contemporary newspapers in the hope of spotting an advertisement for 'Johnson's Bull's Head Brand Gin'. To assist readers in identifying seals not recorded in this book I have added at the end of each section a list of wine merchants, shippers, growers, distillers, and export bottlers who advertised alcoholic drinks sold under brand names in British, American, and Australian newspapers published between 1850 and 1890. The date shown in brackets after each entry on the lists indicates the earliest year for which an advertisement was found during my searches.

Dating sealed bottles The accompanying sketches show the evolution of European wine and spirit bottles from the eighteenth to the nineteenth century. Bottles made before 1820 can be most reliably dated by their general body shape, but after 1820 the question of dating is complicated — in some cases by standardisation; in other cases by a proliferation of bottle makers who produced bottles of all shapes and sizes and who also often re-used earlier designs. The most reliable method of dating a late nineteenth-century sealed bottle which does not carry a date or a label is to ascertain the age of the refuse dump from which the bottle was dug. Fragments of clay tobacco pipes found in such dumps can be dated to within ten years and are of great value in dating associated objects. The bowls and stems are almost always marked with makers' initials which can be checked against dated lists published by many museums in Britain.

When details about the refuse dump are unavailable

collectors should first check the illustrations in this book in the hope of finding a reference to the seal on the bottle. If the seal is illustrated the accompanying information will show the *earliest* year in which the bottle could have been manufactured. Pin-pointing the *actual* year of manufacture is then largely a matter of guesswork, but there are a few additional clues which can be looked for:

On bottles with wide bodies made before 1860 the seal is usually positioned midway between the base and shoulders of the bottle. From 1860 to 1870 many seals were positioned closer to the base of the bottle. After 1870 it was common practice to place the seal on the shoulders of the bottle.

Black glass (i.e. near-opaque brown or dark green) usually indicates a year of manufacture before 1880 for whisky, rum, and brandy bottles and a date before 1870 for wine bottles.

On whisky, rum, and brandy bottles (and on the few beer bottles that have seals) necks became narrower and longer from 1860 to 1880.

On wine bottles shoulders became more rounded after 1870. (Note: Many modern French and German wine bottles have reverted to the shoulderless pre-1870 design.)

Pontil scars can be *generally* taken to indicate a pre-1870 date of manufacture but American collectors, who are accustomed to regarding all non-pontil-scarred bottles as later than 1860, should note that accurate dating of European bottles by their base markings is not yet possible because too little is known about 'nipple pontils', 'pimple pontils', and embossed bases. Many bottles showing these features have been accurately dated by associated dump finds to the 1860s and 1870s. The same dumps have also contained bottles with crude open pontils and others with bare iron pontils.

Three-piece moulded bottles can usually be attributed to the 1860s or 1870s but these mould marks are often found on black glass bottles made in the late 1880s and they are by no means rare on early-nineteenth-century bottles. Those embossed on their bases with the words 'H.Ricketts & Co., Glassworks, Bristol.' can be dated 1821—1853, the years during which this company made black glass bottles before amalgamation with Powell & Filer, another Bristol bottle manufacturing company; but moulded and embossed bottles dating as early as 1790 are not unknown in Britain.

Evolution of bottle shapes 1700—1850

Necks of whisky, rum and
brandy bottles 1860—1880

Shoulders of wine bottles
1860—1870

Examples of seals found on privately-owned bottles in the seventeenth, eighteenth and early nineteenth centuries

E. Remy Martin & Co.,
Cognac, France.

Brandy Manufacturers
First used 1724

John Haurie Nephews,
5 Philpot Lane,
London [England]

Wine Shippers
Reg'd 1879   First used 1739

Nathaniel Johnston & Sons,
Bordeaux, France.

Wine Merchants
Reg'd 1876   First used 1776

Francesco Drioli,
1090 Bastioni Moro,
Zara, Austria.

Liqueur Manufacturer
Reg'd 1899   First used 1780

Anderson & Co.,
25 Holborn,
London [England]

Distillers
Reg'd 1876   First used 1786

Van Vollenhoven & Co.,
Amsterdam,
Holland.

Brewers
Reg'd 1877   First used 1791

Otard, Dupuy & Co.,
Cognac,
France.

Brandy Manufacturers
First used 1796

Chaperon Grangère,
Libourne,
France.

Wine merchants
Reg'd 1876   First used 1807

Gallice & Co.,
Epernay,
France.

Wine Merchants
Reg'd 1888   First used 1808

Perrier-Jouet & Co.,
Epernay, Marne [France]

Wine Merchants
Reg'd 1876   First used 1808

Ruinart, Père et Fils,
Reims, France

Champagne Merchants
Reg'd 1876   First used 1816

P. F. Heering,
Copenhagen,
Denmark.

Manufacturers of Cherry Brandy
Reg'd 1877   First used 1818

Enrique Rivero y O'Neale,
Xerez de la Frontera [Spain]

Wine Importers
Reg'd 1882   First used 1821

Allman & Co.,
Bandor, Cork, Ireland.

Distillers
Reg'd 1890   First used 1825

Lanson, Père et Fils,
Reims,
France.

Wine Growers
Reg'd 1876   First used 1826

Kinahan & Sons,
Dublin [Ireland]

Whisky Merchants
Reg'd 1876   First used 1826

Sandeman, Sons & Co.,
20 St. Swithin's Lane,
London [England]

Wine Shippers
Reg'd 1877   First used 1827

Henry Brett & Co.,
11 Idol Court,
Great Tower Street,
London [England]

Liqueur Manufacturer
First used 1829

R. Thorne & Sons,
Greenock,
Scotland.

Distillers
First used 1831

Charles Jobit & Co.,
Cognac, France.

Brandy Merchant
Reg'd 1877   First used 1832

Kunkelmann & Co.,
Reims,
France.

Champagne Growers
Reg'd 1876   First used 1835

Long Brothers,
Killearn Distillery,
North Britain [Scotland]

Distillers
First used 1836

Alfred de Montebello & Co.,
Marne [France]

Manufacturers of Champagne
Reg'd 1876   First used 1836

Matheus Muller,
Eltville on Rhine,
Germany.

Wine Merchant
Reg'd 1876   First used 1838

William Walker & Sons,
Union Street,
Aberdeen [Scotland]

Wine and Spirit Merchants
Reg'd 1876   First used 1838

Martinez, Gassiot & Co.,
37 Mark Lane,
London [England]

Wine Shippers
Reg'd 1877   First used 1839

Dagonet, Chanoine & Fils,
France.

Champagne Growers
[In use 1840]

Gallice & Co.,
Epernay,
France.

Wine Merchants
Reg'd 1888   First used 1840

Gallice & Co.,
Epernay,
France.

Wine Merchants
Reg'd 1888   First used 1840

Rye Vale Distillery Co. Ltd.,
51 Queen Victoria St.,
London [England]

Distillers
Reg'd 1880   First used 1840

Ruinart, Père et Fils,
Reims, France.

Champagne Merchants
Reg'd 1876   First used 1842

Hog Curtis, Campbell & Co.,
23 Rood Lane,
London E.C. [England]

Wine and Spirit Merchants
Reg'd 1896   First used 1845

Gonzales, Byass & Co.,
3 Brabant Court,
London [England]

Wine Growers & Shippers
Reg'd 1876   First used 1846

Hochheim Wine Association,
(formerly Burgeff & Co.)
Hochheim, Germany.

Manufacturers of Sparkling Wines
Reg'd 1876   First used 1846

Henley & Son,
Tooley Street,
London [England]

Wine and Spirit Merchants
Reg'd 1877   First used 1847

GR

George Roe & Co.,
157 Thomas Street,
Dublin [Ireland]

Distillers
Reg'd 1877   First used 1847

Berry Bros. & Co.,
3 St. James Street,
Westminster,
London [England]

Wine and Spirit Merchants
Reg'd 1876   First used 1848

Frederick W. Cosens,
Jerez, Spain.

Wine Importers
Reg'd 1876   First used 1848

W
D O W

Silva & Cosens,
14 Water Lane,
London [England]

Wine Merchants
Reg'd 1878   First used 1848

W. & J. Mutter,
Bowmore Distillery,
Islay,
Scotland.

Distillers
[In use 1850]

George Claridge,
24 Rood Lane,
London [England]

Wine Merchants
Reg'd 1887   First used 1850

Silva & Cosens,
14 Water Lane,
London [England]

Wine Importers
Reg'd 1876   First used 1850

Charles Heidsieck,
Reims, France.

Champagne Merchants
Reg'd 1876   First used 1850

Quintin Hogg,
23 Rood Lane,
London [England]

Rum Merchants
Reg'd 1883   First used 1850

J. & J. McConnell Ltd.,
Tomb Street,
Belfast [Ireland]

Spirit Merchants
Reg'd 1883   First used 1850

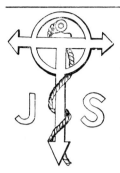

Jerome Saccone Ltd.,
Gibraltar.

Wine Merchants
Reg'd 1892   First used 1850

Jules Mumm & Co.,
82 Mark Lane,
London [England]

Champagne Importers
Reg'd 1876   First used 1851

Offley, Forrester & Co.,
66 Mark Lane,
London [England]

Wine Merchants
Reg'd 1876   First used 1851

Jules Robin & Co.,
Cognac,
France.

Liquor Merchants
Reg'd 1876   First used 1851

Joseph Travers & Sons,
119 Cannon Street,
London [England]

Wine and Spirit Merchants
Reg'd 1881   First used 1851

J. & C. White & Co.,
10 Lime Street,
London [England]

Wine Merchants
Reg'd 1876   First used 1853

John T. Marston,
Poole, Dorset.
[England]

Brewers and Wine and Spirit Merchants
Reg'd 1879   First used 1854

Grimble & Co.,
The Distillery,
Albany Street,
Regent's Park,
London [England]

Distillers
Reg'd 1876   First used 1856

Richard Hooper & Sons,
20 Queenhithe,
London E.C. [England]

Wine Merchants
Reg'd 1876   First used 1856

De St. Marceaux & Co.,
Reims, France.

Champagne Wine Merchants
Reg'd 1876   First used 1856

Veuve Pommery et Fils,
Reims, France.

Wine Merchants
Reg'd 1876   First used 1856

Central Society of Vineyard Proprietors,
Saintes,
Cognac, France.

Wine Merchants
Reg'd 1876   First used 1857

Curlier, Frères & Co.,
Jarnac, France.

Vineyard Proprietors
Reg'd 1876   First used 1857

E. & J. Burke,
16 Bachelor's Walk,
Dublin [Ireland]

Wine & Spirit Merchants
Reg'd 1876   First used 1858

Veuve Planet & Co.,
Cognac,.
France.

Brandy Merchants
Reg'd 1877   First used 1858

Boutelleau & Co.,
Barbeyieux,
France.

Brandy Merchants
Reg'd 1877   First used 1859

Wilmer & Son,
Newport Pagnell,
Buckinghamshire [England]

Brewers and Wine Merchants
Reg'd 1879   First used 1859

Thomas Berry & Co.,
Moorhead,
Sheffield,
Yorkshire [England]

Wine & Spirit Merchants
Reg'd 1876   First used 1860

The European Wine Co.,
Bevis Marks,
St. Mary Avenue,
London [England]

Wine and Spirit Merchants
Reg'd 1879   First used 1860

J. M. Banfield & Co.,
29 Broad Street, Bristol [England]

Wine Merchants
Reg'd 1881   First used 1861

Binet, Fils et Cie,
Reims, France.

Manufacturers of Champagne Wine
Reg'd 1876   First used 1861

Bullock, Lade & Co.,
Glasgow [Scotland]

Distillers
Reg'd 1876   First used 1861

Gabriel Marchand,
Cognac, France.

Brandy Merchants
Reg'd 1876   First used 1861

John Mellor & Co.,
27 Atherton Street,
Liverpool [England]

Wine and Spirit Merchants
Reg'd 1876   First used 1861

Veuve Pommery et Fils,
Reims, France.

Wine Merchants
Reg'd 1876   First used 1861

L. Arnaud,
Cognac, France.

Wine and Spirit Merchants
Reg'd 1876   First used 1862

F. Bernard & Co.,
Reims, France.

Champagne Growers,
Reg'd 1876   First used 1862

Chapman & Wells,
Tanner's Hill,
Deptford, Kent [England]

Wine Merchants
Reg'd 1878   First used 1862

James Eadie,
Cross Street,
Burton on Trent, Staffordshire [England]

Brewers
Reg'd 1877   First used 1863

William Edmonds, Junior & Co.,
Edmund Street, Liverpool [England]

Export Bottlers
Reg'd 1877   First used 1863

Field, Son & Co.,
28 Mincing Lane,
London [England]

Wine and Spirit Merchants
Reg'd 1883   First used 1863

Hutchison & Co.,
Bernard Street,
Leith [Scotland]

Wine & Spirit Merchants
Reg'd 1876   First used 1863

O. F. G.

Robinson, Sanderson & Co.,
11 Quality Street,
Leith [Scotland]

Wine and Spirit Merchants
Reg'd 1884   First used 1863

George Sayer & Co.,
27 Great Tower Street,
London E.C. [England]

Brandy Merchants
Reg'd 1876   First used 1863

CXB

Clode & Baker,
66 Mark Lane,
London [England]

Wine & Spirit Merchants
Reg'd 1876   First used 1864

Charles Coran & Co.,
Cognac,
France.

Brandy Manufacturers
Reg'd 1876   First used 1864

Fisse, Thirion & Co.,
Reims, France.

Wine Merchants
Reg'd 1876   First used 1864

W. Foster Newton & Son,
3 Maiden Lane,
Queen Street,
London E.C. [England]

Wine Merchants
Reg'd 1876   First used 1864

H. J. H. Holdsworth & Co.,
90 Cannon Street,
London E.C. [England]

Wine Merchants
Reg'd 1896   First used 1864

John Mellor & Co.,
27 Atherton Street,
Liverpool [England]

Wine and Spirit Merchants
Reg'd 1876   First used 1864

Theophile Roederer & Co.,
Reims, France.

Champagne Wine Merchants
Reg'd 1876   First used 1864

Société Anonyme de la Distillerie
de la Bénédictine, Liqueur.de l'Abbaye
de Fécamp,
Fécamp, France.

Reg'd 1876   First used 1864

Société Anonyme de la Distillerie
de la Bénédictine, Liqueur de l'Abbaye
de Fécamp,
Fécamp, France.

Reg'd 1876   First used 1864

Société Anonyme de la Distillerie
de la Bénédictine, Liqueur de l'Abbaye
de Fécamp,
Fécamp, France.

Reg'd 1876   First used 1864

A. C. Sonntag,
516 Kingsland Road,
London [England]

Wine and Spirit Merchants
Reg'd 1876   First used 1864

Williams, Jones & Laws,
20½ Great St. Helens,
London [England]

Wine & Spirit Merchants
Reg'd 1877   First used 1864

Brown, Carson & Co.,
15 Guildford Street, Leeds [England]

Wine and Spirit Merchants
Reg'd 1876   First used 1865

Dutton & Co.,
The Brewery,
Warwick [England]

Brewers
Reg'd 1883   First used 1865

R. Finlay Robertson,
12 Narrowgate Street,
Alnwick, Northumberland [England]

Whisky Blenders
Reg'd 1899   First used 1865

Mecke & Meissner,
37 Great Tower Street,
London [England]

Wine Merchants
Reg'd 1877   First used 1865

Mecke & Meissner,
37 Great Tower Street,
London [England]

Wine Merchants
Reg'd 1877   First used 1865

Mecke & Meissner,
37 Great Tower Street,
London [England]

Wine Merchants
Reg'd 1877   First used 1865

The Rhenish Sparkling Wine Co.,
Schierstein on the Rhine,
Germany.

Wine Growers and Merchants
Reg'd 1876   First used 1865

Augier, Frères & Co.,
Cognac, France.

Brandy Shippers
Reg'd 1876   First used 1866

The Birkenhead Brewery Co. Ltd.,
14 Water Street, Liverpool [England]

Brewers and Spirit Merchants
Reg'd 1876   First used 1866

B. B.

William Bolton & Co.,
Westmorland Street,
Dublin [Ireland]

Wine and Spirit Merchants
Reg'd 1876   First used 1866

Fulton, Dunlop & Co.,
Cardiff,
Glamorganshire [Wales]

Wine and Spirit Merchants
Reg'd 1876   First used 1866

Fulton, Dunlop & Co.,
Swansea,
Glamorganshire [Wales]

Wine & Spirit Merchants
Reg'd 1876   First used 1866

A. Miller & Co.,
10/12 Thomas Street,
Dublin [Ireland]

Wine Merchants
Reg'd 1881   First used 1866

Matheus Muller,
Eltville on Rhine,
Germany.

Wine Merchants
Reg'd 1876   First used 1866

David S. Oliver,
Victoria Street,
Bristol [England]

Wine Merchants
Reg'd 1876   First used 1866

Participation Charentaise,
La Grande Marque,
Cognac, France.

Brandy Merchants
Reg'd 1876   First used 1866

Dunville & Co.,
Belfast [Ireland]

Distillers
Reg'd 1877   First used 1867

Koch Fils,
Avize,
Marne, France.

Wine Growers
Reg'd 1876   First used 1867

Lombard de Luc & Co.,
21 Mark Lane,
London E.C. [England]

Wine Shippers
Reg'd 1878   First used 1867

Richardson, Earp & Slater,
Trent Brewery,
Newark on Trent, Nottinghamshire
[England]

Brewers
Reg'd 1882   First used 1867

John Wyndham,
Branxton,
New South Wales,
Australia.

Wine Grower
Reg'd 1885   First used 1867

James D. Brown & Son,
Royal Albert Brewery,
Queen's Road, Reading,
Berkshire [England]

Brewers
Reg'd 1877   First used 1868

L. M. Canneaux et Fils,
Successeurs, Mareuil-sur-Ay,
France.

Champagne Growers and Shippers
Reg'd 1880   First used 1868

Augustus Tribot Fils & Co.,
Cognac, France.

Wine & Spirit Merchants
Reg'd 1876   First used 1868

Robert Brown,
17 Hope Street,
Glasgow [Scotland]

Wine and Spirit Merchants
Reg'd 1886   First used 1869

James Robinson & Son,
30/34 Cloth Market,
Newcastle on Tyne [England]

Wine and Spirit Merchants
Reg'd 1884   First used 1869

J. E. Shand & Co.,
2 Albert Mansions,
Victoria Street,
Westminster, London [England]

Wine Merchants
Reg'd 1879   First used 1869

Bagots, Hutton & Co.,
William Street,
Dublin [Ireland]

Whisky Merchants
[In use 1870]

Louis Napoleon Barron,
Old Compton Street,
London [England]

Wine & Spirit Merchants
Reg'd 1893   First used 1870

John A. Bertram & Co. Ltd.,
7 Quality Street,
Leith [Scotland]

Wine & Spirit Merchants
Reg'd 1898   First used 1870

Boll & Co.,
Reims, France.

Champagne Manufacturers
Reg'd 1881   First used 1870

Bushell Bros. & Co.,
25 Castle Street,
Liverpool [England]

Wine and Spirit Merchants
Reg'd 1877   First used 1870

F. Dessandier & Co.,
Cognac,
France.

Brandy manufacturers
[In use 1870]

Dublin Distillery Co.,
30 Bachelor's Walk,
Dublin [Ireland]

Distillers
Reg'd 1876   First used 1870

William Ford & Sons,
Leith, North Britain [Scotland]

Wine and Spirit Merchants
Reg'd 1882   First used 1870

William Foulds,
Hope Street,
Glasgow [Scotland]

Whisky Merchants
[In use 1870]

William Gillies,
Glendarroch Distillery,
Ardrishaig, North Britain [Scotland]

Distillers
[In use 1870]

Guthrie, Martin & Co.,
Brechin Distillery,
Brechin,
North Britain [Scotland]

Distillers
[In use 1870]

Hau & Co.,
France.

Champagne growers
[In use 1870]

Jonathan Holden,
Reims, France.

Wine Growers and Shippers
Reg'd 1888   First used 1870

Jordan & Co.,
61 Jermyn Street,
St. James, London [England]

Wine Merchants
Reg'd 1876   First used 1870

Thomas Lightfoot,
Well Garth Brewery,
Masham, Yorkshire·[England]

Brewers and Wine Merchants
Reg'd 1877   First used 1870

Low, Robertson & Co.,
Leith [Scotland]

Distillers
[In use 1870]

Donald P. McDonald,
Fort William, North Britain [Scotland]

Distiller
Reg'd 1876   First used 1870

McKenna & Magill,
Academy Street,
Belfast [Ireland]

Whisky Merchants
[In use 1870]

R. Pages & Co.,
Tarragona [Spain]

Wine Shippers
[In use 1870]

Richard Robinson & Sons,
2 Guildhall Street,
Preston, Lancashire [England]

Wine & Spirit Merchants
Reg'd 1887   First used 1870

George Rose,
Millburn Distillery,
Inverness, North Britain [Scotland]

Distillers
[In use 1870]

Ross & Cameron,
Inverness,
Scotland.

Spirit Merchants
Reg'd 1882   First used 1870

George Stapleton,
Market Deeping,
Lincolnshire [England]

Brewers
Reg'd 1878   First used 1870

John Stewart,
87 Fountainbridge,
Edinburgh [Scotland]

Wine and Spirit Merchants
Reg'd 1883   First used 1870

Humphrey Taylor & Co.,
Shawfield Street,
Chelsea,
London [England]

Distillers
Reg'd 1892   First used 1870

Worthington & Co. Ltd.,
Burton on Trent [England]

Brewers and Wine Merchants
Reg'd 1900   First used 1870

James Anderson & Co.,
24 Crutched Friars,
London [England]

Wine Merchants
Reg'd 1876   First used 1871

Alphonse Bellot & Co.,
Cognac, France.

Brandy Bottlers & Shippers
Reg'd 1876   First used 1871

Boisnard, Gonzalez & Co.,
Cognac,
France.

Brandy Merchants
Reg'd 1876   First used 1871

Clifton Juggins James,
30 Great Tower Street,
London [England]

Wine Merchants
Reg'd 1876   First used 1871

Frederick W. Cosens,
Jerez, Spain.

Wine Importers
Reg'd 1876   First used 1871

C. R. Hall & Sons,
17 Dale Street,
Liverpool [England]

Wine and Spirit Merchants
Reg'd 1876   First used 1871

J. & W. Hardie,
4 Picardy Place,
Edinburgh [Scotland]

Wine and Spirit Merchants
Reg'd 1876   First used 1871
(Mark of Boyant & Co., Reims, France.
Champagne Growers)

James Heddle & Co.,
14/17 Mitchell Street,
Leith [Scotland]

Wine & Spirit Merchants
Reg'd 1900   First used 1871

Matthew Hendrie,
78 Wellington Street,
Glasgow [Scotland]

Whisky Distillers
Reg'd 1896   First used 1871

Holliday & Carr,
North Shields,
Northumberland [England]

Ale and Porter Merchants
Reg'd 1883   First used 1871

Lombard de Luc & Co.,
21 Mark Lane,
London E.C. [England]

Wine Shippers
Reg'd 1878   First used 1871

W. H. Marks & Co.,
62/63 Mark Lane,
London E.C. [England]

Wine Merchants
Reg'd 1896   First used 1871

Page & Sandeman,
5½ Pall Mall,
London [England]

Wine and Spirit Merchants
Reg'd 1901   First used 1871

Roullet & Delamain,
Cognac, France.

Vineyard Proprietors,
Reg'd 1890   First used 1871

Toms & Co.,
30 Mark Lane,
London [England]

Wine & Spirit Merchants
Reg'd 1876   First used 1871

Veuve Pommery et Fils,
Reims, France.

Wine Merchants
Reg'd 1876   First used 1871

M. & H. J. Ashby,
The Wine Vaults,
High Street, Staines, Middlesex [England]

Wine and Spirits Merchants
Reg'd 1894   First used 1872

Marie Brizard & Roger,
Bordeaux,
France.

Liquor Merchants
Reg'd 1876   First used 1872

Sidney Clements & Co.,
Queen's Road,
Buckhurst Hill,
Chigwell, Essex [England]

Wine and Spirit Merchants
Reg'd 1876   First used 1872

Edwin Carter Cooper,
Holt, Norfolk [England]

Wine Merchants
Reg'd 1878   First used 1872

Cutler, Palmer & Co.,
3 New London Street,
London [England]

Wine and Spirit Merchants
Reg'd 1877   First used 1872

Cutler, Palmer & Co.,
3 New London Street,
London [England]

Wine and Spirit Merchants
Reg'd 1878   First used 1872

Deutz-Geldermann,
Ay, Marne,
France.

Wine Merchants
Reg'd 1887   First used 1872

Finke & Co.,
27 Clement's Lane, Lombard Street,
London [England]

Wine Merchants
Reg'd 1877   First used 1872

Robert Hillcoat & Sons,
39 Stockwell Street,
Glasgow [Scotland]

Wine and Spirit Merchants
Reg'd 1876   First used 1872

Holt Brothers,
Burnham,
Somerset [England]

Brewers
Reg'd 1888   First used 1872

Hubert Hurter & Son,
Coblenz-on-Rhine,
Germany.

Wine & Spirit Merchants
Reg'd 1876   First used 1872

A. Lalande & Co.,
94 Quai des Chartrons,
Bordeaux, France.

Wine Growers
Reg'd 1888   First used 1872

Morgan Brothers,
38 Trinity Square,
London [England]

Wine Merchants
Reg'd 1881   First used 1872

W. & T. Restell,
29 Mark Lane,
London [England]

Wine & Spirit Merchants
Reg'd 1878   First used 1872

Rouyer, Guillet & Co.,
59 Mark Lane,
London E.C. [England]

Brandy Merchants
Reg'd 1888   First used 1872
(Mark of L. Taillebourg & Co.,
Cognac, France)

Ruck, Fenwick & Ruck,
19 St. Dunstan's Hill,
London [England]

Wine & Spirit Merchants
Reg'd 1880   First used 1872

Henry Stokes & Co.,
King Street,
Snow Hill, London [England]

Distillers and Wine Merchants
Reg'd 1876   First used 1872

Thomas Swift,
Newtown, North Wales.

Brewers and Wine and Spirit Merchants
Reg'd 1885   First used 1872

John Barnett & Son,
36 Mark Lane,
London [England]

Wine Merchants
Reg'd 1877   First used 1873

Booth & Ogden,
Red Cross Brewery,
Rastrick,
Yorkshire [England]

Brewers
Reg'd 1878   First used 1873

Marie Brizard & Roger,
Bordeaux, France.

Liquor Merchants
Reg'd 1876   First used 1873

Marie Brizard & Roger,
Bordeaux,
France.

Liquor Merchants
Reg'd 1876   First used 1873

Comandon & Co.,
Cognac, France.

Brandy Manufacturers
Reg'd 1876   First used 1873

William Edmonds, Junior & Co.,
Edmund Street, Liverpool [England]

Export Bottlers
Reg'd 1877   First used 1873

Ihlers & Bell,
30 Moor Street,
Liverpool [England]

Export Bottlers
Reg'd 1878   First used 1873

Charles Kinloch & Co.,
3 Queen Victoria Street,
London [England]

Wine and Spirit Merchants
Reg'd 1881   First used 1873

Thomas Porter & Sons,
King Street,
Sheffield, Yorkshire [England]

Wine and Spirit Merchants
Reg'd 1876   First used 1873

The Victoria Wine Company,
8/10 Osborn Street,
Whitechapel, Middlesex [London,
England]

Wine and Spirit Merchants
Reg'd 1882   First used 1873

Amiot & Lecluse,
Saumur, France.

Wine Growers
Reg'd 1878   First used 1874

James Anderson & Co.,
24 Crutched Friars,
London [England]

Wine Merchants
Reg'd 1876   First used 1874

Marie Brizard & Roger,
Bordeaux, France.

Liquor Merchants
Reg'd 1876   First used 1874

Brown Corbett & Co.,
30 Victoria Street,
Belfast [Ireland]

Distillers
Reg'd 1883   First used 1874

Wratislaw Henri Czuba,
Cognac,
France.

Brandy Merchants
Reg'd 1876   First used 1874

Duminy & Co.,
Ay
France.

Wine Merchants
Reg'd 1876   First used 1874

William Edmonds, Junior & Co.,
Edmund Street, Liverpool [England]

Export Bottlers
Reg'd 1877   First used 1874

William Jameson & Co.,
Marrowbone Lane,
Dublin [Ireland]

Whisky Distillers,
Reg'd 1876   First used 1874

Lamb & Watt,
46/48 St. Anne Street,
Liverpool [England]

Wine and Spirit Merchants
Reg'd 1876   First used 1874

Launceston & Co.,
17 Store Street,
London [England]

Wine & Spirit Merchants
Reg'd 1887   First used 1874

John McGillchrist Ross,
Jeaninich Distillery,
Alness, Ross-shire [Scotland]

Distillers
Reg'd 1880   First used 1874

J. R. Phillips & Co.,
Nelson Street,
Bristol [England]

Wine and Spirit Importers,
Reg'd 1881   First used 1874

A. J. Riggs & Co.,
76 Great Tower Street,
London [England]

Wine.and Spirit Merchants
Reg'd 1880   First used 1874

Walter Showell,
Crosswells Brewery,
Langley Green, Oldbury,
Worcestershire [England]

Brewers
Reg'd 1880   First used 1874

Charles Watkins,
Imperial Brewery,
Hereford [England]

Brewers and Wine and Spirit Merchants
Reg'd 1880   First used 1874

Underwood & Co.,
55 Sandgate Road,
Folkestone, Kent [England]

Wine Merchants
Reg'd 1892   First used 1874

Underwood Penfold & Co.,
55 Sandgate Road,
Folkestone, Kent [England]

Wine Merchants
Reg'd 1892   First used 1874

OOO
VVV?

Wisdom & Warter,
50 Mark Lane, London [England]

Sherry Shippers,
Reg'd 1878   First used 1874

W.F.A.

William Frederick Attwater,
75 Mark Lane,
London [England]

Wine Merchants
Reg'd 1876   First used 1875

Bernard & Co.,
Leith, North Britain [Scotland]

Distillers
Reg'd 1876   First used 1875

Auguste Billerey,
Beaune, France.

Wine Merchants
Reg'd 1895   First used 1875

Booth's Distillery Ltd.,
55 Cow Cross Street,
London [England]

Distillers
Reg'd 1900   First used 1875

Cavendish, Edinborough & Co.,
4 Callum Street, Fenchurch Street,
London E.C. [England]

Wine and Spirit Merchants
Reg'd 1894   First used 1875
(Mark of Chastaignier & Co., Epernay, France)

W. H. Chaplin & Co.,
10 Villiers Street,
Strand, Middlesex [London, England]

Wine and Spirit Merchants
Reg'd 1888   First used 1875

Child & Co.,
43 Leicester Square, London [England]

Export Bottlers
Reg'd 1877   First 1875

Dublin Whisky Distillery Co.,
Jones Road,
Dublin [Ireland]

Distillers
[In use 1875]

Dunville & Co. Ltd.,
Royal Irish Distilleries,
Belfast [Ireland]

[In use 1875]

Daniel John Fox,
17 Corn Exchange Chambers,
Seething Lane, London [England]

Wine Merchants
Reg'd 1876   First used 1875

C. R. Hall & Sons,
17 Dale Street,
Liverpool [England]

Wine and Spirit Merchants
Reg'd 1876   First used 1875

Holt & Cormack,
6 Great Tower Street,
London [England]

Wine Shippers
Reg'd 1877   First used 1875

Mackie & Gladstone,
88 Hamilton Street,
Birkenhead, Cheshire [England]

Wine and Spirit Merchants
Reg'd 1877   First used 1875

George Morton Ltd.,
24/51 Dock Street,
Dundee [Scotland]

Distillers
Reg'd 1901   First used 1875

E. & W. Pim,
Belfast [Ireland]

Wine and Spirit Merchants
Reg'd 1882   First used 1875

Renault & Co.,
Cognac, France.

Brandy Merchants
Reg'd 1876   First used 1875

Wachter & Co.,
Epernay, France.

Wine Growers
Reg'd 1877   First used 1875

Brockbank & Mellor,
Liverpool [England]

Wine & Spirit Merchants
Reg'd 1876

Louis Eisler,
34 Eastcheap,
London E.C. [England]

Wine Merchants
Reg'd 1876

Jose Bernardo Ferreira,
2 St. Dunstan's Hill,
London [England]

Wine Merchants
Reg'd 1876

S. Hanson, Son, Evison & Barter,
47 Botolph Lane,
London [England]

Wine Merchants
Reg'd 1876

S. Hanson, Son, Evison, & Barter,
47 Botolph Lane,
London [England]

Wine Merchants
Reg'd 1876

Offley, Forrester & Co.,
66 Mark Lane,
London [England]

Wine Merchants
Reg'd 1876

Johannes J. W. Peters,
86 Grunerdeich,
Hamburg, Germany.

Distillers
Reg'd 1876

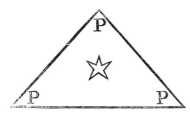

Julio Toscach Ruffier,
98 Leadenhall Street,
London [England]

Wine and Spirit Merchants
Reg'd 1876

Julio Toscach Ruffier,
98 Leadenhall Street,
London [England]

Wine & Spirit Merchants
Reg'd 1876
(Mark of Paul Blanc, Reims)

Thomas Rule,
Harrogate, Yorkshire [England]

Wine Merchants
Reg'd 1876

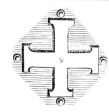

Arthur Southard,
2 St. Dunstan's Hill,
London [England]

Wine Merchants'
Reg'd 1876

Robert Stevenson,
260/262 Buchanan St.,
Glasgow [Scotland]

Wine and Spirit Merchants
Reg'd 1876

William Yaxley,
38/46 London Street,
Norwich [England]

Wine & Spirit Merchants
Reg'd 1876

Birmingham and District Brewery Co. Ltd.,
St. Peter's Place,
Broad Street, Birmingham [England]

Brewers and Wine and Spirit Merchants
Reg'd 1877

J. Brown & Co.,
9 Cazenove Road,
Stoke Newington, London [England]

Wine & Spirit Merchants
Reg'd 1877

Denyer & Co.,
95 Regent Street,
London [England]

Wine Merchants
Reg'd 1877

Edouard Ditely,
Bagnols St. Jean,
France.

Wine Growers
Reg'd 1877

East & Co.,
Maiden Row Brewery,
Louth, Lincolnshire [England]

Brewers
Reg'd 1877

Gray & Co.,
Bathwick Brewery,
Bath, Somerset [England]

Brewers and Wine and Spirit Merchants
Reg'd 1877

John Robertson & Son,
Dundee [Scotland]

Spirit Merchants
Reg'd 1877

Charles J. Smith & Co.,
115 High Street, Camden Town,
Middlesex [London, England]

Wine and Spirit Merchants
Reg'd 1877

Thomas & Hollingworth,
Millstone Lane, Leicester [England]

Wine and Spirit Merchants
Reg'd 1877

James Thorne & Co.,
Stag's Head Brewery,
York Road, Wandsworth,
London [England]

Brewers
Reg'd 1877

J. J. Wickham & Co.,
Stephenson Place,
Birmingham [England]

Wine and Spirit Merchants
Reg'd 1877

Maria Jose Valente Allen,
Oporto, Portugal.

Wine Growers
Reg'd 1878

Robert Bishop & Co.,
6/10 Railway Arches,
Haggerstone Station,
Middlesex [England]

Ale and Porter Merchants
Reg'd 1878

John Burnett & Co.,
Highbridge,
Somerset [England]

Wine and Spirit Merchants
Reg'd 1878

William H. Culshaw,
11 Rumford Place,
Liverpool [England]

Wine & Spirit Merchants
Reg'd 1878

Daniel J. Fox,
17 Corn Exchange Chambers,
Seething Lane, London [England]

Wine Merchants
Reg'd 1878
(Mark of Eville & Fils, Ay, France)

J. R. Parkington & Co.,
24 Crutched Friars,
London [England]

Wine Merchants
Reg'd 1878

W. & T. Restell,
29 Mark Lane,
London [England]

Wine and Spirit Merchants
Reg'd 1878

Ferdinand Rosing,
11 Billiter Square,
London [England]

Wine Merchants
Reg'd 1878

Robert James Thurlow,
7 Flass Street,
Durham [England]

Ale and Porter Merchants
Reg'd 1888   First used 1878

Matthew Mitchell & Son,
1 High Street,
Stoke Newington, Middlesex
[London, England]

Brewers and Wine Merchants
Reg'd 1879

J. A. & H. J. Panton,
Wareham, Dorset [England]

Brewers
Reg'd 1879

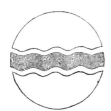

Robert Eadie & Sons,
Blackford,
Scotland.

Brewers
Reg'd 1880

James J. Coverdale,
5 Mark Lane,
London [England]

Wine Merchants
Reg'd 1888   First used 1880

Kelso & Evans,
86 Great Tower St.,
London [England]

Spirit Merchants
Reg'd 1880

Moigneaux Père et Fils,
26 Crutched Friars,
London [England]

Champagne Growers
Reg'd 1880

James Sword & Son,
47 Hutcheson St.,
Glasgow [Scotland]

Wine and Spirit Merchants
Reg'd 1880

Tredell & Co.,
29 Great St. Helen's,
London [England]

Wine & Spirit Shippers
Reg'd 1880

W. J. & T. Welch,
10 Corn Exchange Chambers,
Seething Lane, London [England]

Wine Merchants
Reg'd 1880

Whitmore & Co.,
Downing Street,
Cambridge [England]

Wine Merchants
Reg'd 1880

Edward Archer,
Worcester Road,
Great Malvern,
Worcestershire [England]

Wine and Spirit Merchants
Reg'd 1881

Blood, Wolfe & Co.,
Redcross Street,
Liverpool [England]

Wine and Spirit Merchants
Reg'd 1881

The Consolidated Wine and Spirit Co.,
2A St Peter's Square,
Manchester [England]

Wine and Spirit Merchants
Reg'd 1881

The Crayford Wine & Spirit Stores,
Crayford, Kent [England]

Wine and Spirit Merchants
Reg'd 1881

Archibald Fraser & Son,
31 St. Vincent Place,
Glasgow [Scotland]

Wine and Spirit Merchants
Reg'd 1881

Ackerman-Laurance,
Saint Hilaire,
St. Florent,
France.

Wine Growers
Reg'd 1882

T. S. Biggs & Co.,
Dorchester [England]

Wine Merchants
Reg'd 1882

Coningham & Co.,
11 Regent Street,
London S.W. [England]

Wine and Spirit Merchants
Reg'd 1882

The Distillers Company Ltd.,
Edinburgh [Scotland]

Distillers
Reg'd 1882

Hope & Bendle,
Carlisle, Cumberland [England]

Wine and Spirit Merchants
Reg'd 1882

W. L. Jones & Sons,
10 Longbrook Street,
Exeter [England]

Wine Merchants
Reg'd 1882

The Exors of the Late Henry Joplin,
196/200 London Road,
Liverpool [England]

Wine and Spirit Merchants
Reg'd 1882

Louis A. Nathan,
Dashwood House,
New Broad Street,
London [England]

Spirit Merchants
Reg'd 1882

The North of Spain Vineyard
Proprietors Co.,
Haro, Spain.

Wine Growers
Reg'd 1882

T.A. Shepherd & Co.,
49 Mark Lane,
London [England]

Wine and Spirit Merchants
Reg'd 1882

Short & Co.,
333 Strand, Westminster, London [England]

Wine Merchants
Reg'd 1882

J. Stocks & Co.,
Shibden, Halifax,
Yorkshire [England]

Brewers and Wine and Spirit Merchants
Reg'd 1882

W. Williams & Sons,
Regent Quay,
Aberdeen, North Britain [Scotland]

Wine and Spirit Merchants
Reg'd 1882

Joseph Ansell & Sons,
Park Road,
Aston, Birmingham [England]

Brewers and Wine and Spirit Merchants
Reg'd 1883

Bailey & Co.,
Chertsey Brewery,
Chertsey [England]

Brewers
Reg'd 1883

George Cockburn,
21 Castle Street,
Edinburgh [Scotland]

Wine Merchants
Reg'd 1883

B. Gassies & Co.,
Cognac, France.

Brandy Merchants
Reg'd 1883

I. Gautier & Co.,
Jarnac, Cognac,
France.

Brandy Merchants
Reg'd 1883

Duncan Macpherson & Co.,
14 Renfield Lane,
Glasgow [Scotland]

Wine and Spirit Merchants
Reg'd 1883

Robert Porter & Co.,
77/79 Pancras Road,
London N.W. [England]

Export Bottlers
Reg'd 1883

Stewart Pott & Co.,
Glasgow [Scotland]

Wine and Spirit Merchants
Reg'd 1883

Whitton & Ashley,
Lincoln [England]

Wine and Spirit Merchants
Reg'd 1883

Robert Daniel Wilkinson,
137 High Street,
Borough, London [England]

Wine and Spirit Merchants
Reg'd 1883

The Alasco Wine Co.,
33 Little Queen Street,
Holborn, London [England]

Wine Merchants
Reg'd 1884

Almeida & Co.,
24 Great Tower Street,
London [England]

Wine and Spirit Merchants,
Reg'd 1884

Cantwell & McDonald,
Dublin [Ireland]

Wine and Spirit Merchants
Reg'd 1884

Louis Fabre & Co.,
Reims,
France.

Wine Growers
Reg'd 1884

Hedges & Butler,
155 Regent Street,
London [England]

Wine & Spirit Merchants
Reg'd 1884
(Mark of Melnotte & Fils, Reims, France)

Richard Hooper & Sons,
20/21 Queenhithe,
London E.C. [England]

Wine and Spirit Merchants
Reg'd 1884

W. H. Milner & Co.,
67 King Street,
Manchester [England]

Wine and Spirit Merchants
Reg'd 1884

C. Mitchell & Son,
Brechin, North Britain [Scotland]

Distillers
Reg'd 1884

Ruck & Co.,
19 St. Dunstan's Hill,
London E.C. [England]

Wine and Spirit Merchants
Reg'd 1884

Seligman Bros. & Co.,
20 Bucklersbury, London E.C. [England]

Wine and Spirit Merchants
Reg'd 1884

Stephenson, Rontley & Co.,
42 Cross Street,
Manchester [England]

Wine & Spirit Merchants
Reg'd 1884
(Mark of Louis Fabre & Co.,
Reims, France)

Egidio Vitali,
5/6 Great Winchester Street Buildings,
London [England]

Wine Importers
Reg'd 1884

Thomas Walter & Co.,
Glasgow [Scotland]

Wine and Spirit Merchants
Reg'd 1884

A. S. Watson,
106 Fenchurch Street,
London E.C. [England]

Wine Merchants
Reg'd 1884

James Watson & Co.,
Seagate, Dundee, North Britain
[Scotland]

Whisky Merchants
Reg'd 1884

Robert Brown,
17 Hope Street,
Glasgow [Scotland]

Wine and Spirit Merchants
Reg'd 1885

Alexander Findlater & Co.,
29/31 Upper Sackville Street,
Dublin [Ireland]

Wine and Spirit Merchants
Reg'd 1885

J. & W. Hardie,
Edinburgh [Scotland]

Wine and Spirit Merchants
Reg'd 1885

The Hibernian Distilleries Co.,
51 Middle Abbey Street, Dublin [Ireland]

Wine and Spirit Merchants
Reg'd 1885

Joseph Walton Hope,
44 Lowther Street,
Carlisle, Cumberland [England]

Wine and Spirit Merchants
Reg'd 1885

Julienne & Fils,
2 Riches Court,
Lime Street, London [England]

Wine & Spirit Merchants
Reg'd 1885

Jules Neilson & Co.,
16 Bachelor's Walk,
Dublin [Ireland]

Export Bottlers
Reg'd 1885

James Pettit & Co.,
110 Cannon Street,
London E.C. [England]

Wine and Spirit Merchants
Reg'd 1885

Joseph Francis Quinn,
51 Middle Abbey Street,
Dublin [Ireland]

Wholesale Spirit Dealers
Reg'd 1885

S. Shorter & Co.,
Suffolk House,
Cannon Street,
London [England]

Wine & Spirit Merchants
Reg'd 1885

Taylor & Ferguson,
38 Oswald Street,
Glasgow [Scotland]

Wine and Spirit Merchants
Reg'd 1885

Charles Underhill & Co.,
37 Corn Market Street, Oxford [England]

Wine and Spirit Merchants
Reg'd 1885

J. & T. Usher,
Horfield Road Brewery,
Bristol [England]

Brewers and Wine and Spirit Merchants
Reg'd 1885

James Watson & Co.,
Seagate,
Dundee [Scotland]

Wine and Spirit Merchants
Reg'd 1885

Robert Blair & Son,
Edinburgh [Scotland]

Wine and Spirit Merchants
Reg'd 1886

Boord & Son,
Allhallows Lane,
London [England]

Wine & Spirit Merchants
Reg'd 1886

J. P. Brodie,
Inverness, Scotland.

Wine Merchants
Reg'd 1886

P. B. Burgoyne & Co.,
The Australian Vineyards Association,
6 Dowgate Hill, London E.C. [England]

Wine Merchants
Reg'd 1886

Alex Cairns & Son,
Leith [Scotland]

Wine and Spirit Merchants
Reg'd 1886

Sarah Crocker,
33 Cotham Hill,
Clifton, Bristol [England]

Wine and Spirit Merchants
Reg'd 1886

Davis & Littlewood,
11 Queen Victoria Street,
London E.C. [England]

Wine & Spirit Merchants
Reg'd 1886

Earle, Charrington & Co.,
82/83 Grosvenor Street,
London [England]

Wine and Spirit Merchants
Reg'd 1886

Thomas Foster & Co.,
45 Cheapside, London [England]

Wine Merchants
Reg'd 1886

Robert Goodall Hanson,
Kimberley,
Nottingham [England]

Wine and Spirit Merchants
Reg'd 1886

JJ&S

John Jameson & Son,
Bow Street Distillery,
Dublin [Ireland]

Distillers
Reg'd 1886

George Kirkhope & Son,
Irvine,
North Britain [Scotland]

Whisky Merchants
Reg'd 1886

Edward M. Smith,
59 Mark Lane, London [England]

Wine and Spirit Merchants
Reg'd 1886

Wiley & Co.,
Old Haymarket,
Sheffield, Yorkshire [England]

Wine & Spirit Merchants
Reg'd 1886

William Wilks,
Ashford, Kent [England]

Wine Merchants
Reg'd 1886

The Australian Wine Co.,
4 Mill Street,
Hanover Square,
London W. [England]

Wine Merchants
Reg'd 1887

William Barker & Son,
48/49 Bishopsgate Street Without,
London [England]

Distillers and Wine Merchants
Reg'd 1887

G. Boehm,
Wachenheim,
Germany.

Wine Merchants
Reg'd 1887

Browning, Wood & Fox,
29 Worship Street,
Finsbury, London E.C. [England]

Distillers
Reg'd 1887

Howe & Alexander,
Cromwell Brewery,
Newark on Trent, Nottinghamshire
[England]

Brewers
Reg'd 1887

Kunkelmann & Co.,
(Successors to H. Piper & Co.)
Reims, France.

Champagne Merchants
Reg'd 1887

Pimms & Co.,
3/5 Poultry,
London E.C. [England]

Wine Merchants
Reg'd 1887

Robert W. Rankine,
Rosebank Distillery,
Falkirk, Scotland.

Distillers
Reg'd 1887

James Ainslie & Co.,
201 Leith Walk, Leith,
North Britain [Scotland]

Wine & Spirit Merchants
Reg'd 1888

Nathaniel Antill,
Portsea,
Hampshire [England]

Wine & Spirit Merchants
Reg'd 1888

Bisquit, Dubouche & Co.,
Cognac, France.

Brandy Merchants
Reg'd 1888

Burgis & Colbourne,
Leamington Spa,
Warwickshire [England]

Wine & Spirit Merchants
Reg'd 1888

Ehrmann Bros.,
2 Gresham Buildings,
Basinghall Street,
London, E.C. [England]

Wine Merchants
Reg'd 1888

Carlo Grassi,
40 Gerrard Street, Soho, London [England]

Wine Merchants
Reg'd 1888

John Houlding,
Tynemouth Street,
Everton, Liverpool [England]

Brewers
Reg'd 1888

A. Miller & Co.,
11 Thomas Street,
Dublin [Ireland]

Wine and Spirit Merchants
Reg'd 1888

More & Co. Ltd.,
88 Old Street, St. Luke's,
London E.C. [England]

Brewers and Wine and Spirit Merchants
Reg'd 1888

William Adolph & Co.,
9 Bury Court,
London E.C. [England]

Wine and Spirit Merchants
Reg'd 1890

The Australian Wine Importers Ltd.,
2 East India Avenue,
London [England]

Wine Importers
Reg'd 1890

Central Glenlivet Bonding Co.,
Carncorn, Scotland.

Distillers
Reg'd 1890

Clode & Baker,
66 Mark Lane,
London, E.C. [England]

Wine and Spirit Merchants
Reg'd 1890

Collier & Co.,
53 Southside Street,
Plymouth, Devon [England]

Wine and Spirit Merchants
Reg'd 1890

Compagnie Française, des Eaux de Vie,
L. Teilliard, Paris [France]

Brandy Distillers
Reg'd 1890

William Currie & Co.,
3/7 Elbe Street,
Leith [Scotland]

Whisky Merchants
Reg'd 1890

Delbeck & Co.,
Reims, France.

Wine Merchants
Reg'd 1890

Edwin B. Dive,
113 New Kent Road,
London S.E. [England]

Wine & Spirit Merchants
Reg'd 1890

Duff & Maclaren,
56 Holborn Viaduct,
London [England]

Wine & Spirit Merchants
Reg'd 1890

John Farncombe & Son,
Seaford, Sussex [England]

Wine and Spirit Merchants
Reg'd 1890

Leonid Fedorovitch,
Count von der Pahlen,
Gross Eckau Distillery,
Courland, Russia.

Distillers
Reg'd 1890

Fremy Fils,
Chalonnes sur Loire,
France.

Liqueur Manufacturers
Reg'd 1890

The Gordon Hotels Ltd.,
25 Cockspur Street,
London [England]

Hotel Proprietors and Wine and Spirit Merchants
Reg'd 1890

The Irish Whisky Co. Ltd.,
6 Queen Street,
Belfast [Ireland]

Whisky Merchants
Reg'd 1890

Vincent Legros,
Cannes, France.

Wine Merchants
Reg'd 1890

Levinger & Co.,
Mayence on Rhine,
[Germany]

Wine & Spirit Merchants
Reg'd 1890

Littlejohn Bros.,
3 Sandgate Street,
Ayr, Scotland

Wine & Spirit Merchants
Reg'd 1890

The Maryport Brewery Ltd.,
Maryport,
Cumberland [England]

Brewers
Reg'd 1890

T. Newman & Co.,
31 Marchmont Street,
London [England]

Wine Merchants
Reg'd 1890

The Norman Liqueur Co.,
22 Waverley Street, Hull, Yorkshire
[England]

Liqueur Manufacturers
Reg'd 1890

Rutland & Lett,
63 High Street,
Audley, Worcestershire [England]

Wine Merchants
Reg'd 1890

John Sanderson & Sons,
157 Northumberland Street,
Newcastle on Tyne [England]

Brewers and Wine and Spirit Merchants
Reg'd 1890

George Saunier,
Rouillac,
France.

Wine Merchants
Reg'd 1890

John A. Smith,
2 St. Stephens Place,
Edinburgh [Scotland]

Wine and Spirit Merchants,
Reg'd 1890

The Sparkling Wine Co.,
6/7 Lord Street,
Bewdley, Worcestershire [England]

Wine Merchants
Reg'd 1890

Johann Baptist Sturm,
3 Rheinstrasse, Rudesheim,
Germany.

Wine Merchants
Reg'd 1890

White, Moir & Co.,
32 Bernard Street,
Leith [Scotland]

Wine & Spirit Merchants
Reg'd 1890

John Henry Alcock,
6 Old Market Place,
Grimsby, Lincolnshire
[England]

Wine Merchants
Reg'd 1891

Filleux Brothers,
Cognac, France.

Brandy Merchants
Reg'd 1891

Veuve Louis Pommery,
Reims,
France.

Champagne Merchants
Reg'd 1891

Firth Brothers,
Albert Brewery,
Sutcliffe Street,
Halifax [England]

Brewers and Wine and Spirit Merchants
Reg'd 1893

Henry Burnay,
16 Rue Fanqueiros,
Lisbon [Portugal]

Wine Growers
Reg'd 1893

Gow & Ross,
97 Seagate, Dundee [Scotland]

Whisky Merchants
Reg'd 1893

G. & E. Lefebvre,
37/38 Mark Lane, London E.C. [England]

Distillers
Reg'd 1893

Henry Burnay,
16 Rua Fanqueiros,
Lisbon, Portugal.

Wine Growers
Reg'd 1894

Gerrard & Bartram,
42/43 Welsh Back,
Bristol [England]

Wine Merchants
Reg'd 1894

Alec Mackenzie & Sons,
40 Great Tower Street,
London [England]

Wine & Spirit Merchants
Reg'd 1894

H. & T. Walker,
41 Eastcheap,
London, E.C. [England]

Liqueur Importers
Reg'd 1895

Henri Abele,
48 Rue de la Justice,
Reims, France.

Champagne Shippers
Reg'd 1896

Alexander Duncan & Co.,
97 Seagate, Dundee,
Scotland.

Wine and Spirit Merchants
Reg'd 1896

Jas. McBean & Co.,
45 Hope Street,
Glasgow [Scotland]

Wine and Spirit Merchants
Reg'd 1896

J. McBean & Co.,
45 Hope Street,
Glasgow [Scotland]

Wine and Spirit Merchants
Reg'd 1896

L. C. Richardson & Co.,
13/14 Trinity Square,
London E.C. [England]

Wine and Spirit Merchants
Reg'd 1896

Henkell & Co.,
Mainz on Rhine,
Germany.

Wine Shippers
Reg'd 1899

ADVERTISERS

A list of advertisers whose bottled drinks were mentioned
in newspaper advertisements between 1850 and 1880.
(Sources: The Times (London); The Illustrated London
News; The Sydney Morning Herald (New South Wales); The
New York Times; The New York Herald; The New York
Tribune.)

Adolphe Champagne (1868)
Alt Bros Australian Wines (1870)
Alusse, E., Brandy (1872)
Arbourin, Marett & Co Brandy
(1870)
Arenas, M., Sherry (1861)
Armstrong Gun Whisky (1853)
Ashbourner, J., Biart & Co Wines
(1868)
Ayala & Co Champagne (1880)

Barat, J., Champagne (1876)
Barnett & Fils Brandy (1863)
Barraud Frère Aine & Co Brandy
(1871)
Barraud, Pierre, & Co Brandy
(1874)
Barriason & Co Brandy (1865)
Baxter Barleybee Whisky (1880)
Bechade, Laffont & Co Brandy
(1872)
Bechade, Louis, & Co Brandy
(1854)
Beith Ross Scotch Whisky
(1876)
Bellot, Jules, & Co Brandy
(1856)
Bellot, Lucien, & Co Brandy
(1867)
Bel Oiseau Champagne (1865)
Bernard, Pierre, Champagne
(1871)
Billecart-Salmon Champagne
(1874)
Bisinger Champagne (1878)
Boirot Fils Wines (1870)
Bollinger, J., Champagne (1880)
Bonniot Brandy (1855)
Boutillier, G., Briand & Co
Brandy (1879)

Bouvet-Ladubay Wines (1873)
Bouyer, E., & Co Brandy (1860)
Bovet & Co Champagne (1872)
Bowen & McKechnie Melrose
Old Highland Whisky (1879)
Brett, Henry, & Co Brandy
(1850)
Briand, J., & Co Brandy (1859)
Brown & Pank Whisky (1877)
Bumiller, F., Champagne (1870)
Burdon Sherry (1863)
Bussac, L., & Co Brandy (1875)
Butler Port (1860)

Cameron Inverness Whisky
(1866)
Camuset, Jules, Champagne
(1862)
Canney & Roughton Wines
(1859)
Canot, Charles, & Co Champagne
(1878)
Carcenita Zara Maraschino
(1870)
Carlton Frères Champagne
(1880)
Carmichael Porphyre Hock
(1860)
Catto Whisky (1880)
Central Vineyard Co Brandy
(1865)
Chabanneau, Pierre, Wines
(1870)
Champagne Vineyard
Proprietors Champagne (1860)
Champion, Jules, (1863)
Chandros Champagne (1878)
Chanoine Frères Champagne
(1877)
Chartreuse Liqueur (1860)

Château & Co Brandy (1871)

Château de Conde Champagne (1871)

Cinzano, Francesco & Co Vermout di Torino (1879)

Class, F., & Co. Wines

Claudon, Gustave, Brandy (1868)

Cliquot, Eugene, Champagne (1865)

Cliquot, Henri, Champagne (1865)

Cliquot, Madame, Champagne (1860)

Clouzeau Brandy (1860)

Cognac Brandy Association Brandy (1861)

Collin, Adolphi, Champagne (1868)

Collins L'Universal Champagne (1860)

Cork Distillery Whisky (1870)

Courvoisier Brandy (1859)

Cozen Masonic Sherry (1850)

D'Ali & Bordonaro Wines (1873)

Dalwood Australian Wines (1872)

Damour, Leonce, Brandy (1873)

Danieud, I., Fils & Co Brandy (1876)

D'Arcy Old Irish Whisky (1878)

Davies Sherry (1880)

Dawson Whisky (1879)

De Cazanova, C., Champagne (1874)

De Freycinet & Fils Champagne (1874)

Deinhard Hock (1879)

De Laage Fils & Co Brandy (1871)

De Lacourt Champagne (1879)

De Luze & Son Claret (1868)

De Marcilly Frères Burgundy (1870)

De Montiguy & Co Champagne (1878)

Denis & Maune Brandy (1860)

Desbordes, Xavier, & Fils Champagne (1867)

Dessaudier Champagne (1867)

De St Marceau & Co Champagne (1865)

De Venage & Co Champagne (1871)

Dhu, Roderick, Scotch Whisky (1875)

Doignon, A., Fils & Co Brandy (1864)

Donaldson, Robert, & Co Port (1876)

Donaldson, Robert, & Co Wines (1969)

Drouet & Co Champagne (1867)

Drouillard, A., & Co Brandy (1864)

Dubois, Alfred, Lizee & Co Brandy (1880)

Dubois Fils & Co Brandy (1878)

Dubois Frères & Cagnion Brandy (1880)

Ducasse, L., & Co Brandy (1869)

Dufaut & Co Champagne (1877)

Duff, Gordon & Co Sherry (1873)

Dulary Brandy (1870)

Dumecq, Peter, Sherry (1860)

Dupanloup & Co Champagne (1869)

Dupont, J., & Co Brandy (1876)

Dupuy & Fils Champagne (1867)

Duret, Gustave, & Co Brandy (1867)

Erbach Hock (1870)

Ernest Champagne (1879)

Ettamogah Colonial Wines (1869)

Exshaw Brandy (1867)

Fallon Colonial Wines (1875)

Farre, Charles, Champagne (1876)

Faure, J., Brandy (1878)

Fenn Colonial Wines (1880)

Ferrari Zara Maraschino Liqueur (1870)

Fettercairn Whisky (1880)
Flambeau Champagne (1856)
Fockink Curaçao Liqueur (1855)
Fockink Manarine Liqueur
(1855)
Foley, Richard, Irish Whisky
(1872)
Forest & Belleau Champagne
(1873)
Foucauld, Lucien, & Co Brandy
(1864)
Fournier, Jules, Champagne
(1873)
Fournier, V., & Co Brandy
(1871)
Frapin, P., & Co Brandy (1864)
Freminet & Fils Champagne
(1870)
Fremy-Ronce, A., Wines (1864)
Fromy & Rogee Brandy (1861)
Furlaud, George, & Co Brandy
(1870)

Gaine, W.A., & Co. Kentucky
Hermitage Bourbon Whisky
(1880)
Garnier, J., Abricotine Liqueur
(1868)
Garnier, J., Curaçao Liqueur
(1868)
Garnier, J., French Anisette
Liqueur (1868)
Garnier, J., Liqueur d'Or (1868)
Garnier, J., Zara Maraschino
Liqueur (1870)
Garvey Sherry (1860)
Gibbon Irish Malt Whisky (1850)
Giesler & Co Champagne (1871)
Gilbey Castle Brand Scotch
Whisky (1865)
Gillon, John, & Co Mountain
Dew Whisky (1878)
Glencairn Whisky (1879)
Glen Para Colonial Wines (1870)
Goulet, Georges, & Co Champagne
(1869)
Graham, W. & J., Port (1867)
Gratien, Alfred, Wines (1868)

Greenlees Bros Lorne Whisky
(1875)
Groffier-Todd Burgundy (1870)
Guerin Frères Brandy (1872)
Guinefollaud, L., Brandy (1870)

Hardy, A., & Co Champagne
(1867)
Hautier Brandy (1868)
Hennessy & Co Champagne
(1855)
Hennessey Battleaxe Brandy
(1872)
Henriot Champagne (1871)
Henriot & Co Champagne (1868)
Hine, T., & Co Champagne (1867)
Hopkin, J., & Co Whisky (1880)
Hotalong Bourbon Whisky (1875)
Hunt, Roope, Teage & Co Port
(1871)
Huvet & Co Champagne (1871)

Irroy, Ernest, & Co Champagne
(1869)
Iverson, R., Sherry (1871)

Jacquesson Champagne (1870)
Jeben Sherry (1880)
Johnson Colonial Claret (1874)
Jopp, W. & K., Malt Whisky
(1868)
Jules Champagne (1867)

Kemp & Co Whisky (1865)
Krug & Co Champagne (1865)
Kurz & Co Champagne (1871)

Laffont, George, & Co Brandy
(1873)
La Grande Marque Brandy (1860)
Lagrillère Champagne (1871)
Laidlow & Sandeman Whisky
(1876)
La Rose Claret (1879)
Laurant, Eugene, & Co
Champagne (1871)
Lebegue & Co Brandy (1879)
Lecluse, A.J., Wines (1860)
Le Forestier, A., & Fils
Champagne (1867)

Lemon Hart Rum (1855)
Leoville Claret (1879)
Lepelletier Absinthe (1865)
Lichwitz Brandy (1867)
Lima & Fils Champagne (1868)
Lochnager Whisky (1880)
Lock, John, Irish Whisky (1880)
Lorvain, Jules, Wines (1865)
Lowndes Rum (1850)
Low, Robertson & Co Diamond
Brand Whisky (1879)
Luxardo Zara Maraschino
Liqueur (1850)

Macfarlane Old Still Whisky
(1870)
Macholl Frères Liqueur (1868)
Mackenzie Dalmore Whisky
(1869)
Magazzin Zara Maraschino
Liqueur (1870)
Mahalm, William, & Co Irish
Whisky (1878)
Maison Berton Champagne (1871)
Marcellain Brandy (1873)
Marcobrunn Hock (1860)
Marett Brandy (1869)
Marquis de Bleu Wines (1867)
Martell & Co Brandy (1855)
Martineau, Gustave, Brandy
(1860)
Martini, Sold & Co Vermouth
(1871)
Masdeu Port (1865)
Mason Old Scotch Malt Whisky
(1872)
Matignon, A., & Co Brandy
(1860)
Maurice Brandy (1872)
Max Sutaine & Co Champagne
(1868)
Melnotte et Fils Champagne
(1879)
Mercier & Co Champagne (1878)
Mestreau & Co Brandy (1860)
Meukow & Co Brandy (1870)
Midlothian Scotch Whisky (1880)

Millilich Zara Maraschino
Liqueur (1870)
Misa, M., Sherry (1865)
Moet & Chandon Champagne
(1860)
Mola Zara Maraschino Liqueur
(1870)
Moreaux & De Neuville Wines
(1865)
Morgan Bros Port (1879)
Muro Wines (1862)

Nierstein Hock (1872)
Noilly Pratt Absinthe (1870)
Normandin, E., & Co Brandy
(1870)
Normandin, Maignen & Co Wines
(1868)
Noyeau Liqueur (1870)

Ogg Old Strathdee Whisky (1878)

Palmer, R.R., & Co Cheviot
Brand Whisky (1871)
Pauillac Claret (1879)
Pellisson, J.E., & Co Brandy
(1871)
Pellisson Père & Co Brandy
(1865)
Peneau & Co Champagne (1871)
Pereire, Jules, Champagne (1861)
Père Kerman Liqueurs (1869)
Perigeux & Co Champagne (1872)
Perinet & Fils Champagne (1880)
Petrot-Bonnet Champagne (1871)
Pfungst Frères & Co Champagne
(1876)
Pinet, Castillon & Co Brandy
(1870)
Piper & Co Champagne (1858)
Planet, Veuve & Co Brandy
(1862)
Pol Roger & Co Champagne
(1860)
Pommery & Greno Champagne
(1860)
Preller Green Label Claret (1875)
Preston Irish Whisky (1880)

Preston, R.W., Rum (1868)
Prunier, J. & Co Brandy (1873)

Queen & Co Sherry (1867)
Quenardel-Vieville Champagne (1878)
Quillet, O., & Co Brandy (1871)

Ranson & Co Brandy (1867)
Raynal & Co Brandy (1866)
Reuss, Lautern & Co Burgundy (1870)
Richot & Co Brandy (1850)
Rivière, Gardrat & Co Brandy (1880)
Rizat Brandy (1870)
Rochegrise Brandy (1868)
Roper Frères Champagne (1879)
Rota Zara Maraschino Liqueur (1870)
Roughton Port (1863)
Rousse, Jules, Brandy (1864)
Rousteaux Wines (1867)
Roux & Bazin Brandy (1860)
Roy, G., & Co Brandy (1871)
Rumpff & McShane Champagne (1876)

Sayer, George & Co Brandy (1871)
Sazerac, De Forge & Sons Brandy (1863)
SCPV Brandy (1867)
Sequin, V., Emile & Co Brandy (1876)
Sime, E., & Co Brandy (1872)
Sorin Brandy (1860)
Southern Vineyard Proprietors Wines (1869)
St Emilion Claret (1872)
St Estephe Claret (1868)
St Gervais Claret (1871)
St Julien Claret (1870)
St Marceaux & Co Brandy (1872)
St Mungo Blend Scotch Whisky (1879)
St Verdelot & Co Brandy (1876)
Stampali Zara Maraschino

Liqueur (1870)
Stewart & Co Kirkliston Whisky (1879)
Stibbe, H., Curaçao (1868)
Strauss Champagne (1876)

Taragona Port (1871)
Teacher, William & Sons Whisky (1868)
Teggart, H., Irish Whisky (1872)
Testulat-Brouleau Champagne (1880)

Thom & Cameron Whisky (1879)
Thoreau, E., & Fils Wines (1879)
Tricoche & Co Brandy (1879)
Turnbull & Wood Glen Brand Whisky (1878)
Twiss & Browning Rum (1868)

Uam Var Scotch Whisky (1880)
United Vineyard Proprietors Brandy (1867)

Valres & Co Champagne (1867)
Verrier, A., Jeune & Co Champagne (1871)
Vignier, Evariste & Co Brandy (1869)
Vincent & Pugh Ginger Brandy (1872)
Vine Growers Co of Cognac Brandy (1879)
Voillot, A., Burgundy (1876)

Walker, A., Whisky (1878)
Watt, A.A., & Co Irish Whisky (1876)
Williams & Co Scotch Whisky (1876)
Wilson, A., Tochineal Whisky (1879)
Wilson, James, & Son Bann Brand Irish Whisky (1879)
Wright & Greig Whisky (1870)
Wright & Partridge Wines (1876)
Young & King Belfast Irish Whisky (1880)
Yvon, A., & Co Brandy (1872)

2. CASE GINS AND SCHNAPPS

Hollands, Geneva, Schiedam, Netherlands Spirit — by whatever name it was known Dutch gin smelled as sweet to large numbers of Englishmen, Americans, Australians, and South Africans in the nineteenth century. The square, tapered, olive green bottles in which it was shipped are found in their thousands in the old refuse dumps of these countries and most collectors have a dozen or more different specimens on their display shelves. It is not known exactly when this vast export business first began but it is certainly known that Dutch gin distillers were among the first to use sealed bottles as commercial containers. Bottles bearing seals impressed with their trade marks have been found by marine archaeologists in Dutch wrecks dated as early as 1700. Indeed the very shape of the bottle, achieved by free-blowing into an open-ended wooden former, was evolved to meet the needs of an industry anxious to improve its export packaging. It was obviously much quicker and cheaper to make simple square crates to carry a dozen square glass bottles than it was to protect in transit the round, saltglazed Flemish 'bellarmines' in which gin was bottled in the Middle Ages.

Little is known about the early history of the industry because the bottle collecting hobby and its associated activities, dump digging and historical research into container history, have not yet achieved popularity in Holland. What is known from digging evidence brought to light in Britain, the United States, Australia, and South Africa is that in the 1870s there were more than twenty internationally famous distillers mainly concentrated in the Dutch town of Schiedam. All of them used pictorial or monogram seals on their bottles and many of them also manufactured schnapps — gin flavoured with aromatic herbs — and bottled it in straight-sided square bottles which were always embossed but rarely carried shoulder seals. All of the bottles — gin and schnapps — were by that time mould-blown and had applied lips. Earlier specimens dating from 1860 and before were hand-blown and of much cruder body shape with open pontils. The practice of applying seals to those case gins used by the Schiedam distillers lingered into the twentieth century, as is proved by the finding in Britain and Australia of one or two specimens with mould seams passing through the lip of the bottle.

Although Holland took the lion's share of the market in gin in the nineteenth century other countries were involved with the industry. There were a few distillers in Germany and Belgium and a fair number in Britain, especially in London and Plymouth where locally-made gin had an international reputation at least equal to Dutch rivals. The British manufacturers also used square bottles but they were more often embossed than shoulder sealed. Sloe gin, a very popular drink in those days, was England's equivalent to Dutch schnapps.

Readers are reminded that *embossed* gin and schnapps bottles may not carry the *complete* trade mark as shown in the following illustrations which, in some cases, show labels which were registered as trade marks.

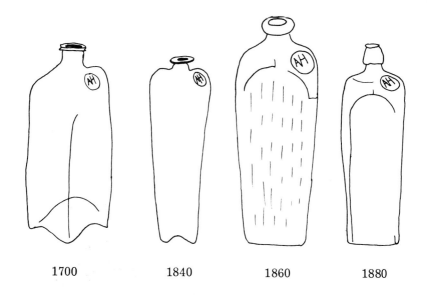

1700   1840   1860   1880

Evolution of case gins 1700—1880

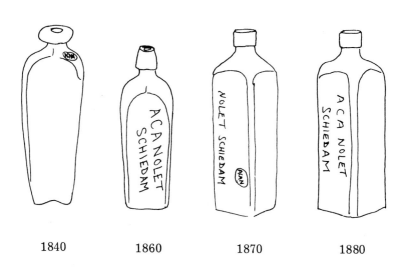

1840   1860   1870   1880

Evolution of schnapps bottles 1840—1880

Coates & Co.,
Black Friars' Gin Distillery,
Plymouth, Devon [England]

Distillers
First used 1793

Ball & Dunlop,
Rotterdam, Holland.

Distillers
Reg'd 1876   First used 1821

J. H. Henkes,
Delftshaven, Holland.

Distillers
Reg'd 1876   First used 1826

J. H. Henkes,
Delftshaven, Holland.

Distillers
Reg'd 1876   First used 1826

John De Kuyper & Son,
Rotterdam, Holland.

Distillers
Reg'd 1876   First used 1826

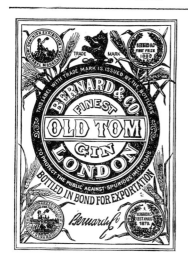

Bernard & Co.,
Leith, Scotland.

Distillers
Reg'd 1886   First used 1843

Vanden Bergh & Co.,
Antwerp, Belgium.

Distillers
Reg'd 1876   First used 1843

J. S. Smith, Druce & Co.,
Phoenix Distillery,
London [England]

Distillers
Reg'd 1886   First used 1846

J. & W. Nicholson & Co.,
St. John Street,
Clerkenwell, London [England]

Distillers
Reg'd 1890   First used 1850

J. H. Henkes,
Delftshaven, Holland.

Distillers
Reg'd 1876   First used 1851

Koninklijke Nederlandsche Fabrick van
Likeuren,
Amsterdam, Holland.

Liqueur Manufacturers
Reg'd 1878   First used 1853

Grimble & Foster,
Albany St., London.

Wine and Spirit Merchants
Reg'd 1893   First used 1856

J. H. Henkes,
Delftshaven, Holland.

Distillers
Reg'd 1876   First used 1858

Jan Hendrik Henkes,
Delftshaven, Holland.

Distillers
Reg'd 1876   First used 1858

Van Dulken, Weiland & Co.,
Rotterdam, Holland.

Distillers
Reg'd 1891   First used 1860

J. H. Henkes,
Delftshaven, Holland.

Distillers
Reg'd 1876   First used 1861

J. H. Henkes,
Delftshaven, Holland.

Distillers
Reg'd 1876   First used 1862

E. Kiderlen,
Delftshaven,
Rotterdam, Holland.

Distillers
Reg'd 1891   First used 1862

A. A. Watt & Co.,
14 Ship Quay St.,
Londonderry, Ireland.

Wine and Spirit Merchants
Reg'd 1876   First used 1866

A. Scott & Co.,
46 Fish Street Hill,
London [England]

Gin Importers
Reg'd 1882   First used 1867

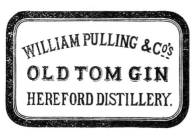

William Pulling & Co.,
The Hereford Distillery,
Hereford, England.

Distillers
Reg'd 1896   First used 1868

Hills & Underwood,
25 Eastcheap,
London E.C. [England]

Distillers
Reg'd 1876   First used 1869

James Anderson & Co.,
24 Crutched Friars,
London [England]

Wine and Spirit Merchants
Reg'd 1876   First used 1869

Erven Lucas Bols,
Distillery 't Lootsje,
Amsterdam, Holland.

Distillers
Reg'd 1875

Johannes Theodorus Beukers,
Schiedam, Holland.

Distillers
Reg'd 1876

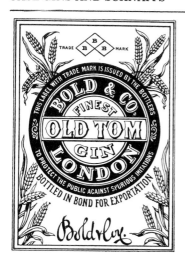

Bold & Co.,
9 Yardheads, Leith, Scotland.

Distillers
Reg'd 1886

Wiley & Co.,
Old Haymarket,
Sheffield, Yorkshire [England]

Wine and Spirit Merchants
Reg'd 1887

J. B. Groen Gz.,
Amsterdam, Holland.

Distillers
Reg'd 1887

De Nederlandsche Gist-En Spiritus
Fabrick,
Delft, Holland.

Distillers
Reg'd 1890

Herman Jansen,
Langehaven,
Schiedam, Holland.

Gin Refiners and Exporters
Reg'd 1890

Pieter Loopuyt & Co.,
Schiedam, Holland.

Spirit Merchants
Reg'd 1890

Hulstkamp & Zoon & Molyn,
Rotterdam, Holland.

Distillers
Reg'd 1890

W. H. Chaplin & Co.,
10 Villiers Street,
Strand, London [England]

Wine and Spirit Merchants
Reg'd 1896

H.M. Ffennell & Co.,
180 Western Road,
Brighton [England]

Wine and Spirit Merchants
Reg'd 1898

Charles Bunting Ltd.,
High Street,
Uttoxeter, Staffordshire [England]

Wine and Spirit Merchants
Reg'd 1898

J. R. Phillips & Co. Ltd.,
19 Nelson Street,
Bristol [England]

Distillers
Reg'd 1899

The following illustrations show seals
found on case gins owned by members of
The British Bottle Collectors' Club.

Arnold Cornelius Alorsius Nolet,
Schiedam, Holland.

Distillers
[In use 1850]

A. van Hoboken,
Rotterdam, Holland.

Distillers
[In use 1850]

C. W. Herwig,
Schiedam,
Holland.

Distillers
[In use 1860]

Palboom C. Meyer & Co.,
Schiedam, Holland.

Distillers
[In use 1860]

Blankenheym & Nolet,
Rotterdam, Holland.

Distillers
[In use 1870]

L. Eisler & Co.,
Berlin, Germany.

Distillers
[In use 1870]

P. Hoppe,
Schiedam, Holland.

Distillers
[In use 1870]

P. Loopuyt & Co.,
Schiedam, Holland.

Distillers
[In use 1870]

Palboom C. Meyer & Co.,
Schiedam, Holland.

Distillers
[In use 1870]

Netherlands Yeast & Spirit Manufactory

[In use 1870]

Netherlands Yeast & Spirit Manufactory

[In use 1870]

Netherlands Yeast & Spirit Manufactory

[In use 1870]

A. C. A. Nolet,
(Las Armas Brand)
Schiedam, Holland.

Distillers
[In use 1870]

Arnold Cornelius Alorsius Nolet,
Schiedam, Holland.

Distillers
[In use 1870]

Someren Greve & Co.,
(Double Anchor Brand)
Schiedam, Holland.

Distillers
[In use 1870]

Stein Brothers,
Berlin, Germany.

Distillers
[In use 1870]

Stein Brothers,
Berlin, Germany.

Distillers
[In use 1870]

Unknown mark on Dutch case gin bottles

[Circa 1870]

Unknown mark on Dutch case gin bottles

[Circa 1870]

W. P. Zoom,
Schiedam, Holland.

Distillers
[In use 1870]

Blankenheym & Nolet,
Rotterdam, Holland.

Distillers
[In use 1875]

Blankenheym & Nolet,
Rotterdam, Holland.

Distillers
[In use 1875]

Joel Burke Wolfe,
New York, U.S.A.

Manufacturers of Aromatic Schnapps
[In use 1880]

Pictorially embossed case gins
J. J. Melchers,
Schiedam, Holland.

[In use 1880]

Pictorial Embossing on case gins
C. W. Herwig (Corkscrew Brand)
Schiedam, Holland.

[In use 1875]

ADVERTISERS

A list of gin and schnapps distillers and merchants mentioned in newspaper advertisements between 1850 and 1880. (Sources as for previous list)

Boord & Son Gin (1875)

Coates & Co Original Plymouth Gin (1860)

Diment & Co Plymouth Gin (1875)

Gayen Genuine Schiedam Schnapps (1860)
Gilbey & Co Jubilee Schnapps (1887)
Gilbey & Co Silverstream Gin (1870)
Gordon, C., & Co Old Tom (1868)

Holland & Co Gin (1880)

Kahlbaum, C.A.F., (Berlin) German Spirit (1875)
Kiderlen Schnapps (1850)

Lediard Knickerbocker Schnapps (1875)

Meyer & Co Schiedam Schnapps (1872)
Mueller & Co Goldwater Schnapps (1868)

Netherlands Distillery Square Schnapps (1875)

Pimm & Co Old Tom (1868)

Queen Wilhelmina Brand Schnapps (1880)

Radicke, Carl, (Berlin) German Spirit (1865)

Sir Robert Burnett & Co Gin (1875)
Swain, Boord & Co Old Tom (1865)

Tangueray, Charles, & Co Gin (1868)
Tecker, Jan, Geneva (1872)

Van Berckel & Co (Delft) Schiedam (1870)
Van Diepen & Co Schiedam Schnapps (1870)
Van Felman, A., Schnapps (1871)
Vickers, J. & J., & Co Gin (1873)
Volmar Schnapps (1878)

Ware & Schmitz Van Dunk Genever [figural bottle in shape of coachman] (1870)
White Cross Aromatic Schnapps (1870)
Wolfe & Hart Imperial Schiedam (1860)
Wolfe, Udolpho, Aromatic Schiedam Schnapps (1868)

3. BITTERS

The practice of selling alcoholic drinks thinly disguised as
medicine achieved enormous popularity in the United
States in the late nineteenth century. A few bitter tasting
herbs and other 'secret ingredients' were added to gin and
whisky and the resulting brew, which got its name from its
taste, was bottled and sold as a remedy for every known
complaint and malady. The success of the quacks who sold
the stuff was due partly to a heavy tax on liquor from which
'medicines' were exempted and mainly to the powerful
voices of social reformers who attacked hard drinking as
the great evil of the day. The campaigning of these 'do-
gooders' eventually achieved Prohibition, but in the
nineteenth century their activities helped to increase rather
than reduce the amount of alcohol consumed in the United
States and because the 'secret ingredients' in bitters often
included opium and other addictive drugs thousands of
Americans became alcoholics while trying to cure stomach
upsets and ingrowing toenails!

Collecting bitters bottles is probably the most popular
branch of the hobby in the United States where more than a
thousand different specimens are known. In Europe only a
few dozen brands were on sale in the late nineteenth century,
though it is a fact that the first bitters were manufactured
and sold in England in the eighteenth century. The habit
never achieved the same popularity as in the United States
but it lingers to this day in Britain where pink gin — made
by adding Angostura bitters to the alcohol — is still ordered
in public houses. In spite of the few specimens found in
European dumps bitters bottles are appreciated by collectors
on this side of the Atlantic because the bottles are almost
always of attractive shape and colour. American collectors
also appreciate the European specimens they find or buy; they
will no doubt find the following list of more than fifty
British and German bitters and those American brands also
sold in Europe of great interest.

Newcomers to bottle collecting — who will, I hope, read
my earlier books on the subject, listed at the beginning of
the book — should note that bitters bottles are almost
always embossed and only very rarely carry seals. One of

the exceptions is the Hartwig Kantorowicz bitters bottle
shown on the front cover, which bears a seal showing a
star and fish which are also seen on the label (page 125).
Most bitters bottles labels were very ornate. Embossing on
the bottles was usually limited to a few words. For example,
the 'Khoosh Bitters' bottle has only the word 'Khoosh'
embossed on its shoulders. (See label, page 127).

Hubert Underberg-Albrecht,
Rheinberg, Germany.

Alcoholic Bitters Manufacturers
Reg'd 1875   First used 1835

Lemon Hart & Co.,
79 Great Tower Street,
London [England]

Wine and Spirit Merchants
Reg'd 1877   First used 1857

Marie Brizard & Roger,
Bordeaux, France.

Liquor Merchants
Reg'd 1876   First used 1870

BOILING
BITTERS

William C. Hebden,
64 Northgate,
Halifax, Yorkshire [England]

Wholesale Druggists
Reg'd 1883   First used 1871

Hartwig Kantorowicz,
6 Wronker Strasse,
Posen, Germany.

Bitters Manufacturers
Reg'd 1878   First used 1872

Simon & Whelon,
65 Lower Thames St.,
London [England]

Orange Bitters Merchants
Reg'd 1899   First used 1873

Alfred King,
118 Church Street,
Croydon, Surrey [England]

Chemists
Reg'd 1875

Charles M. Fletcher,
72 William St.,
New York, U.S.A.

Patent Medicine Merchants
Reg'd 1878

Winter & Emanuel,
18 Milton Street,
Dorset Square,
London [England]

Bitters Manufacturers
Reg'd 1879

Cantrell & Cochrane,
Nassau Place,
Dublin [Ireland]

Mineral and Aerated Waters Manufacturers
Reg'd 1880

Henry Davis & Co.,
12 Goree Piazzas,
Liverpool [England]

Bitters Manufacturers
Reg'd 1880

T. P. Griffin & Co.,
London [England]

Bitters Manufacturers
Reg'd 1880

The Globe Co.,
193 Commercial Road,
Glasgow [Scotland]

Bitters and Mineral Water Manufacturers
Reg'd 1882

Theodor Lappe,
Neudietendorf, Gotha,
Germany.

Wine Merchants
Reg'd 1883

De Rojas Bros. & Co.,
24/26 Basinghall St.,
London E.C. [England]

Wine and Spirit Merchants
Reg'd 1883

CHIRETTA
TONIC
BITTERS

Thomas T. Edwards,
24 City Buildings,
Old Hall Street,
Liverpool [England]

Bitters Manufacturers
Reg'd 1883

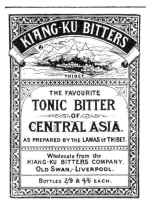

Kiang-Ku Bitters Co.,
1 Ellison Street,
Old Swan,
Liverpool [England]

Bitters Manufacturers
Reg'd 1884

Harold Senier,
88 Norwood Road,
London S.E. [England]

Chemists
Reg'd 1884

Ernst L. Arp,
Kiel, Germany.

Bitters Manufacturers
Reg'd 1885

DOIG'S BLOOD BITTERS

Alexander Doig,
10 Brownswood Park,
London N. [England]

Bitters Manufacturers
Reg'd 1887

MOONSEED ∴ BITTERS.

A. E. Powell & Co.,
Manor House, Swindon,
Wiltshire [England]

Bitters Manufacturers
Reg'd 1888

MILITARY BITTERS

Joseph Hobson & Sons,
Dantzic Brewery,
Leeds, Yorkshire [England]

Bitters Manufacturers
Reg'd 1890

Page & Sandeman,
5½ Pall Mall,
London S.W. [England]

Wine Merchants
Reg'd 1893

Aubrey F. Spencer,
20 Montpelier Crescent,
Brighton, Sussex [England]

Bitters manufacturers
Reg'd 1894

John Taylor,
Perfection Hop Bitters Brewery,
76 Pollard Street,
Manchester [England]

Reg'd 1895

S. B. Sketch & Co.,
Sunny Hill Brewery,
Johnston,
Pembrokeshire [Wales]

Hop Bitters and Mineral Water
Manufacturers
Reg'd 1896

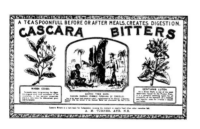

Andrew M. Turner,
Newton Brewery,
Ayr [Scotland]

Alcoholic Bitters Manufacturers
Reg'd 1896

McKendrick, Clark & Co.,
Neilston,
Renfrewshire [Scotland]

Aromatic Bitters Manufacturers
Reg'd 1898

Stower's British & Foreign Wine Co.,
36/38 Commercial Street,
London [England]

Bitters Manufacturers
Reg'd 1898

Monterey Bitters Ltd.,
140 Gray's Inn Road,
London [England]

Bitters Manufacturers
Reg'd 1898

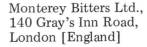

J.J.W. Peters,
50 Grünerdeich,
Hamburg, Germany.

Bitters Manufacturers
Reg'd 1899

John A. Simson,
158 Cromwell Road,
London [England]

Alcoholic Bitters Manufacturers
Reg'd 1899

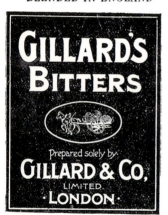

Gillard & Co. Ltd.,
The Vintry Works,
Walthamstow, Essex [England]

Bitters Manufacturers
Reg'd 1901

The Medical and General Specialities Co.,
300 Clapham Road,
London S.W. [England]

Tonic Bitters Manufacturers
Reg'd 1901

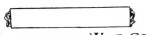

THE TOKENHOUSE WINE CO.
3 TOKENHOUSE BUILDINGS,
LONDON, E.C.

The Tokenhouse Wine Co.,
3 Tokenhouse Buildings,
London E.C. [England]

Wine Merchants
Reg'd 1901

Munyon's Homeopathic Home Remedy
Co.,
53rd and Jefferson Streets,
Philadelphia, U.S.A.

Bitters Manufacturers
Reg'd 1902

William E. Tyrer,
76 Pine Street,
New York, U.S.A.

Aromatic Bitters Manufacturers
Reg'd 1902

ADVERTISERS

A list of European bitters and American bitters sold overseas mentioned in newspaper advertisements between 1850 and 1880.
(Sources as for previous lists)

African Stomach Bitters (1879)
American Cocktail Bitters (1878)
Atwood Bitters (1879)

Birresbon Bitters (1872)
Blankenheym Aromatic Bitters (1876)
Boord Orange Bitters (1880)
Boston Malt Bitters (1876)

California Fig and Herb Bitters (1874)

Dennler Iron Bitters (1875)
Dennler Swiss Alpine Bitters (1871)
Drake Bitters (1876)
Dr Bell Bitters (1878)
Dr Doyle Hop Bitters (1878)
Dr Ralay Royal Digestive Bitters (1873)
Dr Soule Hop Bitters (1878)

Elliot Bros Queensland Hop and Dandelion Bitters (1875)

Fockink Dutch Orange Bitters (1878)
Frisco Hop Bitters (1879)

Garnier, J., Dutch Orange Bitters (1875)
Gauly Baltimore Bitters (1877)

Gipsland Hop Bitters (1880)
Goldwater Dutch Orange Bitters (1879)

Hostetter Bitters (1880)

Jaap, J., Bitters (1875)

Kent Hop Bitters (1876)

Lediard Stomach Bitters (1880)

Meyer Bitters (1880)

New York Hop Bitters (1876)

Orange Bitters (1873)

Philadelphia Hop Bitters (1878)
Pomegranate Bitters (1873)
Pomeranza Bitters (1880)

Queensland Hop Bitters (1880)

Rowland Alkaline Bitters (1850)

Stibbe, H., Orange Bitters (1870)
Stoughton Bitters (1879)

Utica Bitters (1879)

Van Bergh Hop Bitters (1872)

Warner Safe Bitters (1878)
Wolfe Aromatic Bitters (1877)

XLL Bitters (1874)

FURTHER READING

The following magazines are recommended to all who take an interest in bottle collecting:

Old Bottles and Treasure Hunting
801 Burton Road, Burton-on-Trent, Staffordshire, England

Old Bottle Magazine
Box 243, Bend, Oregon 97701, USA

Australian Bottle Review
PO Box 245, Deniliquin, New South Wales 2710, Australia

International Bottle Traders' Gazette
104 Harwal Road, Redcar, Cleveland, England

SUBJECT INDEX

This index is designed to help collectors identify *pictorial* seals on their bottles quickly and easily. Seals which depict only the initials or the name of the bottle merchant are excluded. In those cases the index of firms' names will prove more helpful.

musical instrument, 23, 24, 44,
57, 66, 79, 90
mythical creature, 15, 26, 33,
42, 46, 49, 58, 59, 62, 69,
76, 81, 86, 91, 106, 107

plant,
flower, 66, 105, 132
fruit, 19, 44, 53, 65, 72, 115,
128, 133, 135
other, 41, 48, 51, 55, 60, 65,
72, 70, 79, 106, 108, 112,
117, 118, 125, 127, 129, 130,
131

shield, 15, 18, 19, 21, 25, 30,
32, 36, 37, 41, 44, 47, 49,
53, 54, 60, 68, 69, 71, 73, 77,
86, 90, 91, 94, 135
ship, 56, 79
star,
5-pointed, 17, 19, 23, 25, 27,·
28, 34, 35, 48, 49, 51, 54,
55, 61, 63, 68, 70, 75, 77, 82,
85, 86, 87, 117, 119, 125
6-pointed, 31
other, 26, 81
sun, 33, 57

weapon, 15, 18, 27, 30, 37, 40,
43, 53, 62, 65, 68, 73, 88, 90,
94
wheel, 69, 73, 77,
wing, 23, 49, 68, 73, 74, 88, 90

INDEX OF FIRMS' NAMES